PROVERBS

Learning to Live Wisely

10 STUDIES FOR INDIVIDUALS OR GROUPS

LifeGuide®
BIBLE STUDIES

WILLIAM MOUSER

IVP Connect

An imprint of InterVarsity Press
Downers Grove, Illinois

InterVarsity Press
P.O. Box 1400, Downers Grove, IL 60515-1426
www.ivpress.com
email@ivpress.com

InterVarsity Press® *is the book-publishing division of InterVarsity Christian Fellowship/USA*®, *a movement of students and faculty active on campus at hundreds of universities, colleges and schools of nursing in the United States of America, and a member movement of the International Fellowship of Evangelical Students. For information about local and regional activities, visit intervarsity.org.*

LifeGuide® *is a registered trademark of InterVarsity Christian Fellowship.*

All Scripture quotations, unless otherwise indicated, are taken from the Holy Bible, New International Version®. NIV®. *Copyright* ©*1973, 1978, 1984 by International Bible Society. Used by permission of Zondervan Publishing House. All rights reserved.*

Cover image: ©*Dirk Wustenhagen / Trevillion Images*

ISBN: 978-8308-3026-8

Printed in the United States of America ∞

g **green**
press
INITIATIVE
As a member of the Green Press Initiative, InterVarsity Press is committed to protecting the environment and to the responsible use of natural resources. To learn more, visit greenpressinitiative.org.

| **P** | *31* | *30* | *29* | *28* | *27* | *26* | *25* | *24* | *23* | *22* | *21* |
| **Y** | *29* | *28* | *27* | *26* | *25* | *24* | *23* | *22* | *21* | *20* | |

Contents

GETTING THE MOST OUT OF *PROVERBS* ——————— 5

1 Proverbs 9   **The Choice** ——————*11*

2 Proverbs 7   **The Simple** ——————*16*

3 Proverbs 13:19; 17:12;   **Avoiding the Fool** ——————*21*
18:2, 7; 20:3; 26:11

4 Proverbs 13:10, 20; 14:12;   **Finding Wisdom** ——————*26*
15:12; 21:30; 25:12

5 Proverbs 6:12-14; 16:30;   **Bad Words** —————— *31*
17:4; 18:8; 26:23; 29:5

6 Proverbs 10:19; 15:23; 16:24;   **Good Words**——————*36*
17:10; 24:26; 25:11-12

7 Proverbs 6:6-8; 13:4; 15:19;   **The Sluggard** ——————*41*
22:13; 24:30-34; 26:14-16

8 Proverbs 10:4, 15, 22; 13:8;   **Wealth & Poverty** ——————*46*
18:11, 23; 19:4; 21:6; 30:8-9

9 Proverbs 14:21, 31; 19:6,   **Giving** ——————*51*
17; 21:13

10 Proverbs 11:3; 14:12; 15:22;   **Planning the Future**——————*55*
16:9; 21:5, 31; 27:1

Leader's Notes——————*58*

Getting the Most Out of *Proverbs*

Each year thousands of books published in America have titles with the same first two words: "How to . . ." By reading these books you can learn how to get a job, a federal grant, a divorce, free publicity, a mortgage or even a nightclub gig. You can read about how to buy a car, a house, a small business or a personal computer. You can become a balloon artist, an astrologer, an athlete, a golfer, a fashion designer, a good dancer, a pilot, a master manipulator, a mechanic or a vampire. Experts out there will make you an expert at petting a cat, picking lottery numbers, losing five pounds fast, building fences or bearing children.

All these books offer us wisdom—skill in one area or another. Books like these proliferate because we all need wisdom to live successfully. Wisdom brings success and prosperity in our work, in dealings with family and friends, and in our relationship with God. One book of the Bible—the Proverbs of Solomon—specializes in wisdom. It gives us direction and guidance that is practical, concrete, reasonable, wholesome, understandable, shrewd and fruitful. By reading it we gain skill in all areas of life.

Where Did the Book of Proverbs Come From?

The book of Proverbs begins with the notice "The Proverbs of Solomon, Son of David, King of Israel." This does not mean, however, that Solomon authored every word of the book. In 1 Kings 4:32 we learn that Solomon "spoke three thousand proverbs." Undoubtedly he composed a substantial number of these proverbs himself.

First Kings 4:34 mentions that kings of surrounding nations sent delegations to hear Solomon's wisdom. On the other hand, an exchange of wisdom must have developed between Solomon and those who came to learn from him. The book of Proverbs reflects this interchange. Approximately three hundred proverbs are labeled "The Proverbs of Solomon" in Proverbs 10:1—22:16. Perhaps this section formed the nucleus of the collection. Some years later King Hezekiah's scribes added about 130 additional Solomonic proverbs, found in Proverbs 25:1—29:27. "Sayings of the Wise" appear in Proverbs 22:17—24:22, followed by "More Sayings of the Wise" in Proverbs 24:23-34. Then come "Sayings of Agur" in Proverbs 30:1-33, "Sayings of King Lemuel" in Proverbs 31:1-9 and the acrostic poem on the virtuous wife in Proverbs 31:10-31. Clearly the book of Proverbs as it comes to us contains a diverse collection of proverbs, from a diversity of wise men and at least one woman who is identified as King Lemuel's mother.

Comparing the book of Proverbs with other ancient Near Eastern wisdom literature sheds light on how the collection arose in the first place. In order to instruct their sons, court officials in many lands would pull together the wisdom they had acquired in a lifetime of diplomatic service. From Egypt we have at least ten such collections, from *The Instruction of Ka-gemni* and *The Instruction of Prince Hor-dedef*, dating from the Old Kingdom (2686-2160 B.C.), to *The Instruction of Onchsheshonqy* in the fourth or fifth century B.C. An Akkadian translation of a Sumerian original titled *The Instructions of Shurruppak* dates from approximately 1300 B.C. Ahiqar, who served as vizier to the Assyrian kings Sennacherib and Esarhaddon in the seventh century B.C., left the *Words of Ahiqar*. *The Proverbs of Solomon, Son of David, King of Israel*, takes its place alongside these and other collections. Prophetic authorities added Solomon's proverbs to the canon of Scripture. A manual of instruction for the king's son became available to all of God's children.

What Will Solomon's Proverbs Do for Me?

Solomon tells us the purpose of the collection in Proverbs 1:2-6:

> for attaining wisdom and discipline;
> for understanding words of insight;
> for acquiring a disciplined and prudent life,
> doing what is right and just and fair;
> for giving prudence to the simple,
> knowledge and discretion to the young—
> let the wise listen and add to their learning,
> and let the discerning get guidance—
> for understanding proverbs and parables,
> the sayings and riddles of the wise.

This study guide will introduce you to selected proverbs from Solomon's collection, grouped together under ten different themes. Study questions will guide your thoughts as you ponder the meanings of the proverbs and as you learn to live more wisely.

Suggestions for Individual Study

1. As you begin each study, pray that God will speak to you through his Word.

2. Read the introduction to the study and respond to the personal reflection question or exercise. This is designed to help you focus on God and on the theme of the study.

3. Each study deals with a particular passage—so that you can delve into the author's meaning in that context. Read and reread the passage to be studied. The questions are written using the language of the New International Version, so you may wish to use that version of the Bible. The New Revised Standard Version is also recommended.

4. This is an inductive Bible study, designed to help you discover for yourself what Scripture is saying. The study includes three types of questions. *Observation* questions ask about the basic facts: who, what, when, where and how. *Interpretation* questions delve into the meaning of the passage. *Application* questions help you discover the implications of the text for growing in Christ. These three keys unlock the treasures of Scripture.

Write your answers to the questions in the spaces provided or in a personal journal. Writing can bring clarity and deeper understanding of yourself and of God's Word.

5. It might be good to have a Bible dictionary handy. Use it to look up any unfamiliar words, names or places.

6. Use the prayer suggestion to guide you in thanking God for what you have learned and to pray about the applications that have come to mind.

7. You may want to go on to the suggestion under "Now or Later," or you may want to use that idea for your next study.

Suggestions for Members of a Group Study

1. Come to the study prepared. Follow the suggestions for individual study mentioned above. You will find that careful preparation will greatly enrich your time spent in group discussion.

2. Be willing to participate in the discussion. The leader of your group will not be lecturing. Instead, he or she will be encouraging the members of the group to discuss what they have learned. The leader will be asking the questions that are found in this guide.

3. Stick to the topic being discussed. Your answers should be based on the verses which are the focus of the discussion and not on outside authorities such as commentaries or speakers. These studies focus on a particular passage of Scripture. Only rarely should you refer to other portions of the Bible. This allows for everyone to participate in in-depth study on equal ground.

4. Be sensitive to the other members of the group. Listen attentively when they describe what they have learned. You may be surprised by their insights! Each question assumes a variety of answers. Many questions do not have "right" answers, particularly questions that aim at meaning or application. Instead the questions push us to explore the passage more thoroughly.

When possible, link what you say to the comments of others. Also, be affirming whenever you can. This will encourage some of the more hesitant members of the group to participate.

5. Be careful not to dominate the discussion. We are sometimes so eager to express our thoughts that we leave too little opportunity for others to respond. By all means participate! But allow others to also.

6. Expect God to teach you through the passage being discussed and through the other members of the group. Pray that you will have an enjoyable and profitable time together, but also that as a result of the study you will find ways that you can take action individually and/or as a group.

7. Remember that anything said in the group is considered confidential and should not be discussed outside the group unless specific permission is given to do so.

8. If you are the group leader, you will find additional suggestions at the back of the guide.

^{1}Wisdom has built her house;
  she has hewn out its seven pillars.
^{2}She has prepared her meat and mixed her wine;
  she has also set her table.
^{3}She has sent out her maids, and she calls
  from the highest point of the city.
^{4}"Let all who are simple come in here!"
  she says to those who lack judgment.
^{5}"Come, eat my food
  and drink the wine I have mixed.
^{6}Leave your simple ways and you will live;
  walk in the way of understanding.

^{7}"Whoever corrects a mocker invites insult;
  whoever rebukes a wicked man incurs abuse.
^{8}Do not rebuke a mocker or he will hate you;
  rebuke a wise man and he will love you.
^{9}Instruct a wise man and he will be wiser still;
  teach a righteous man and he will add to his learning.

^{10}"The fear of the LORD is the beginning of wisdom,
  and the knowledge of the Holy One is understanding.
^{11}For through me your days will be many,
  and years will be added to your life.
^{12}If you are wise, your wisdom will reward you;
  if you are a mocker, you alone will suffer."

^{13}The woman Folly is loud;
  she is undisciplined and without knowledge.
^{14}She sits at the door of her house,
  on a seat at the highest point of the city,
^{15}calling out to those who pass by,
  who go straight on their way.
^{16}"Let all who are simple come in here!"
  she says to those who lack judgement.
^{17}"Stolen water is sweet;
  food eaten in secret is delicious!"
^{18}But little do they know that the dead are there,
  that her guests are in the depths of the grave.

PROVERBS 9

1

The Choice

An invitation to dinner is always welcome, until you get invitations to two different dinners, each held at the same time as the other. Then you have to decide which one to accept and which one to decline. No doubt you'll make your decision based on many factors—the reputation of the host and hostess, the prospects for a good time, your own tastes in people and food.

GROUP DISCUSSION. When have you had to make a difficult choice between two social events? How did you make the decision?

PERSONAL REFLECTION. What difficulties do you have in facing choices? Is it ever a struggle for you to say no? Why or why not?

Proverbs 9 presents the dilemma of deciding between two dinner invitations. But these are no ordinary dinners, and the invitations come from no ordinary hostesses. Which one you attend will largely determine your health, your wealth and your happiness for the rest of your life. *Read Proverbs 9.*

1. Describe Lady Wisdom's feast.

Describe Woman Folly's feast.

---

2. Do Lady Wisdom and Woman Folly invite the same people or different people to their feasts? Explain.

---

3. Do you think you're among those specifically invited to Lady Wisdom's dinner? Explain.

---

4. Do you think Lady Wisdom would welcome the mocker of verses 7-8? Why or why not?

---

5. What resources does each hostess have to offer her guests?

6. Which hostess appears to offer the most pleasure to her guests? Explain.

7. What do verses 7-12 tell us about how Lady Wisdom imparts benefits to her guests?

8. After reading verse 10, do you think that knowledge and understanding must be explicitly Judeo-Christian in order to be genuine? Why or why not?

9. Proverbs 9 is, of course, an extended metaphor—an allegory. Wisdom is like a wealthy woman inviting guests to a feast. Who embodies the person of Lady Wisdom in their relationship to you?

10. How (in what situations or with which people) have you encountered Woman Folly?

11. No matter which "invitation" you accept, your decision will result in both pleasure and pain. How do the pleasure and pain from dining at Lady Wisdom's house differ from the pleasure and pain one finds at Woman Folly's abode?

12. What helps you to choose wisdom?

Pray that you would leave your "simple ways" and be made worthy of dinner with Lady Wisdom.

Now or Later

Reflect more on Proverbs 9:6. What attitudes or habits do you have that might be classified as "simple"? Make this a matter of prayer and reflection, asking God to reveal true wisdom to you.

^{1}My son, keep my words
and store up my commands within
you.
^{2}Keep my commands and you will live;
guard my teachings as the apple of
your eye.
^{3}Bind them on your fingers;
write them on the tablet of your
heart.
^{4}Say to wisdom, "You are my sister,"
and call understanding your kins-
man;
^{5}they will keep you from the adulter-
ess,
from the wayward wife with her
seductive words.

^{6}At the window of my house
I looked out through the lattice.
^{7}I saw among the simple,
I noticed among the young men,
a youth who lacked judgment.
^{8}He was going down the street near
her corner,
walking along in the direction of
her house
^{9}at twilight, as the day was fading,
as the dark of night set in.

^{10}Then out came a woman to meet him,
dressed like a prostitute and with
crafty intent.
^{11}(She is loud and defiant,
her feet never stay at home;
^{12}now in the street, now in the
squares,
at every corner she lurks.)
^{13}She took hold of him and kissed him
and with a brazen face she said:

^{14}"I have fellowship offerings at home;

today I fulfilled my vows.
^{15}So I came out to meet you;
I looked for you and have found
you!
^{16}I have covered my bed
with colored linens from Egypt.
^{17}I have perfumed my bed
with myrrh, aloes and cinnamon.
^{18}Come, let's drink deep of love till
morning;
let's enjoy ourselves with love!
^{19}My husband is not at home;
he has gone on a long journey.
^{20}He took his purse filled with money
and will not be home till full moon."

^{21}With persuasive words she led him
astray;
she seduced him with her smooth
talk.
^{22}All at once he followed her
like an ox going to the slaughter,
like a deer stepping into a noose
^{23} till an arrow pierces his liver,
like a bird darting into a snare,
little knowing it will cost him his
life.

^{24}Now then, my sons, listen to me;
Pay attention to what I say.
^{25}Do not let your heart turn to her
ways.
or stray into her paths.
^{26}Many are the victims she has brought
down;
her slain are a mighty throng.
^{27}Her house is a highway to the
grave,
leading down to the chambers of
death.

2

The Simple

P. T. Barnum was fond of saying, "A sucker is born every minute." From Solomon's point of view, every one of us was born "simple," that is, gullible, credulous, naive. But while Barnum saw human gullibility as an opportunity for profit, the proverbs see the condition as a character weakness to be corrected. All around us people appeal to our gullibility in one area or another. If we're to escape with our money, health and integrity intact, we need to develop what the proverbs call prudence.

GROUP DISCUSSION. Young children are naive or simple in all areas of life. But all of us remain naive or simple in some areas. Why does this happen, and do you find it to be positive or negative to be naive?

PERSONAL REFLECTION. In what ways do you think you are naive? Do you feel good or bad about this?

The first practical step to wisdom is to identify the simpleton in ourselves. The proverbs in this study are a mirror that lets us see where and how we are naive. And more than that, they will set us on the road to wisdom. *Read Proverbs 7.*

1. How do verses 1-5 and 24-27 provide a frame for this passage?

_____

2. Describe the scene set in verses 6-13.

_____

3. Put yourself in the place of the young man here. What factors make this a tempting situation?

_____

4. What does the seductress say that is probably true (vv. 14-19)?

What does she say (or imply) that is actually false?

_____

5. Men and women "without judgment" can be persuaded to do foolish things other than adultery. Following the logic of the seductress, give another example of how someone could be persuaded to do something foolish.

6. Does the warning in verses 24-27 seem overly dramatic to you? Why or why not?

7. Proverbs 14:15 says, "A simple man believes anything, but a prudent man gives thought to his step." Proverbs 27:12 says, "The prudent see danger and take refuge, but the simple keep going and suffer for it." How are these proverbs about the simpleton exemplified in the young man in Proverbs 7?

8. All of us have spheres of living where we, like the simpleton in Proverbs 7, have little choice but to believe what we are told. What are some of these areas in your life?

How could you gain more wisdom in those areas?

9. Consider a practical project we all face from time to time—buying a car. What "dangers" (Proverbs 27:12) might you face as you proceed?

What should you do to "take refuge" from them without abandoning the project?

What consequences might you suffer if you don't take precautions?

---

10. It's one thing to know we're naive in this or that respect and quite another to develop the character strength called prudence. What can you begin doing now that will make you more prudent in the future?

Jesus said, "Be as shrewd as snakes and as innocent as doves" (Matthew 10:16). Pray for wisdom like that.

Now or Later

Read Proverbs 14:18, 19:25 and 21:11. What else do you learn about gaining wisdom from these passages?

A longing fulfilled is sweet to the soul,
but fools detest turning from evil. (Proverbs 13:19)

Better to meet a bear robbed of her cubs
than a fool in his folly. (Proverbs 17:12)

A fool finds no pleasure in understanding
but delights in airing his own opinions. (Proverbs 18:2)

A fool's mouth is his undoing,
and his lips are a snare to his soul. (Proverbs 18:7)

It is to a man's honor to avoid strife,
but every fool is quick to quarrel. (Proverbs 20:3)

As a dog returns to its vomit,
so a fool repeats his folly. (Proverbs. 26:11)

3

Avoiding the Fool

Proverbs 27:22 makes one very clear point about fools—they're incorrigible:

> Though you grind a fool in a mortar,
>   grinding him like grain with a pestle,
>   you will not remove his folly from him.

But if fools can't be reformed, why do we find such an abundance of proverbs about them? The answer is simple—to help us recognize fools and their foolish behavior, and to warn us about the consequences of both.

GROUP DISCUSSION. Fools have a powerful capacity to cause calamity, not only for themselves but for others as well. Our greatest danger from foolish people comes when we fail to recognize them (or their folly) until it is too late. Describe a situation you've seen where someone is "ambushed" by another person's folly.

PERSONAL REFLECTION. Think of a time when you were ambushed by a foolish person's folly. In hindsight, can you think of any warning signs that you missed, warnings that you're now more sensitive to?

Scattered all through the book of Proverbs are individual proverbs which describe characteristics of the fool. Defensive driving techniques protect us from foolish drivers. The proverbs in this study are some of those in Solomon's wisdom that equip us for "defensive living." *Read the proverbs selected for this study.*

1. Try the "thought experiment" suggested by Proverbs 17:12. Imagine yourself walking in the forest. Now imagine that a rampaging mother bear, robbed of her cubs, comes crashing through the brush. How do you think that situation is like meeting a fool in the midst of his folly?

2. Can you relate an episode from your own life or from the experience of someone you know where encountering a fool was similar to meeting a bear robbed of her cubs?

3. Proverbs 18:2 tells us that fools are always ready with a viewpoint and ever eager to broadcast it. How would you expect a prudent or wise person to behave differently? Give an example.

4. What does proverbs 18:7 suggest might serve as a "fool detector?"

5. How does Proverbs 18:2 explain why Proverbs 18:7 is true?

6. In Proverbs 13:19, the second line would be better translated using the word *so* instead of *but*. What does this change of translation suggest about the fool?

7. Proverbs 20:3 shows us another warning sign about fools— their quickness to quarrel. Think of someone you've observed who acts like this. Why do you think their quickness to quarrel is a good predictor of their folly?

8. Proverbs 26:11 is Solomon's version of a cartoon—a grotesque image with a caption underneath it! What is it about a fool that makes him or her like the dog in the "cartoon"?

9. Jesus warned, "Do not judge, or you too will be judged" (Matthew 7:1). When we use the proverbs about the fool to decide that this or that person is foolish, are we ignoring Jesus' warning? Why or why not?

---

10. Look back over the proverbs to see which of these characteristics remind you of yourself. Describe something you can do this week to guard yourself against foolish behavior.

After his warning about judging others, Jesus said, "Why do you look at the speck of sawdust in your brother's eye and pay no attention to the plank in your own eye?" Pray that you can follow Solomon's advice about fools while heeding Jesus' warning against pride.

Now or Later

Read Matthew 7:1-6. Jesus' advice in verse six is similar to the advice Solomon gives us about foolish people. How is Jesus' advice in verses 1-5 compatible with what he says in verse 6?

Pride only breeds quarrels,
    but wisdom is found in those who take advice. (Proverbs 13:10)

He who walks with the wise grows wise,
    but a companion of fools suffers harm. (Proverbs 13:20)

There is a way that seems right to a man,
    but in the end it leads to death. (Proverbs 14:12)

A mocker resents correction;
    he will not consult the wise. (Proverbs 15:12)

There is no wisdom, no insight, no plan
    that can succeed against the LORD. (Proverbs 21:30)

Like an earring of gold or an ornament of fine gold
    is a wise man's rebuke to a listening ear. (Proverbs 25:12)

4

Finding Wisdom

Proverbs 13:10, 20; 14:12
15:12; 21:30; 25:12

A factory manager's assembly line was down, so he summoned a consultant to suggest remedies. After inspecting a huge piece of machinery, the consultant produced a small hammer, reached between some gears and gave a small tap. The assembly line worked again, and the factory manager got a bill for $10,000. Aghast, the manager demanded another bill itemizing the charges. When it came, the second bill read:

Tapping with hammer: $5.00

Knowing where to tap: $9,995.00

Wisdom is "knowing where to tap." If we don't know where to tap, we need to find someone who does.

GROUP DISCUSSION. Describe a skill you would like to acquire because it would make your life, work or relationships with others better than they are. *Patience, Listen,*

PERSONAL REFLECTION. What skills have your mentors (parents, teachers, coaches) helped you with in the past? *Slow down Listen appreciate person*

The book of Proverbs shows us "where to tap" in many areas of life and also encourages us to seek out those who understand things we cannot yet perceive. *Read the selected proverbs.*

---

1. All these proverbs are pointing, in one way or another, to a single kind of "source" for wisdom. How would you describe that source?

---

2. As you look over these proverbs, what do you see in them that keeps a person from becoming wise? *pride.*

---

3. Think of a mentor or teacher or coach who helped you become wise in some area. Which of the proverbs for this study comes closest to matching how you acquired skill or wisdom from the mentor? Explain your response.

" walks w/ wise grows wise"
seek people, books, shows — from
Godly sources

---

4. In Solomon's day, the wisdom of Proverbs was probably taught in two places—the home and wisdom schools. Today the "wisdom school" takes many forms, from apprenticeships in trade unions to enrollment in universities. Using the proverbs for this study as a guide, what would you look for when trying to select such a school? *✓ Basic — back ground*

5. Of course, formal schooling isn't the only way to get wisdom. Think of a person within your circle of acquaintances who has wisdom that you do not have. How would you describe his or her area of wisdom?

Gentle council, example.

6. What specific steps might you take to acquire the wisdom from that wise man or woman?

mirror

7. Sometimes acquiring wisdom will feel unpleasant. How do the proverbs above explain why "wising up" can sometimes involve pain?

growing pains

8. A common proverb among athletes striving for skill says "No pain, no gain." Give an example from your own life—not involving athletic training—where learning wisdom cost you something in terms of personal pain.

"friendships"

9. Why do you think there is often such a huge gulf between what seems right to us and what is truly wise (Proverbs 14:12)?

can lead to our spiritual death

10. Proverbs 21:30 assures us that certain kinds of advice will come to nothing. How can you know if the advice you've gotten is the kind that will not succeed?

Bible/Godly based

11. The group discussion question asked you to list an area in which you need wisdom. What can you do in the week ahead to begin acquiring it?

Take time to listen~
act to God nudges~

Wisdom, skill, common sense, moxey—whatever you call it, it's something we cannot acquire all by ourselves. We are always standing on the shoulders of wise men and women who lived before us. Pray that in your life you can harvest the wisdom offered by others.

Now or Later

We often say that someone is "street smart," meaning that the person has become "shrewd through enrollment in the School of Hard Knocks." Is this way of gaining wisdom the same as or different from the ways suggested in the proverbs for this study?

A scoundrel and villain,
  who goes about with a corrupt mouth,
  who winks with his eye,
  signals with his feet
  and motions with his fingers,
  who plots evil with deceit in his heart—
  he always stirs up dissension. (Proverbs 6:12–14)

He who winks with his eye is plotting perversity;
  he who purses his lips is bent on evil. (Proverbs 16:30)

A wicked man listens to evil lips;
  a liar pays attention to a malicious tongue. (Proverbs 17:4)

The words of a gossip are like choice morsels;
  they go down to a man's inmost parts. (Proverbs 18:8)

Like a coating of glaze over earthenware
  are fervent lips with an evil heart. (Proverbs 26:23)

Whoever flatters his neighbor
  is spreading a net for his feet. (Proverbs 29:5)

5

Bad Words

**Proverbs 6:12-14; 16:30;
17:4; 18:8; 26:23; 29:5**

A childhood taunt says, "Sticks and stones may break my bones, but words will never hurt me." The sentiment may be brave, but we know from painful memory that words can hurt a lot. Solomon's proverbs speak straightforwardly of the harm that can come from words alone. And yet for all their power to work evil, bad words can be surprisingly (and disconcertingly) pleasant to hear or to speak! What is worse, some of the most damaging words we hear may be ones never "intended" to attack us directly.

GROUP DISCUSSION. All of us have probably stood in the checkout line of a grocery store reading the lurid headlines on the tabloids. Why do you think the tabloids are so "appealing" to the casual bystander?

PERSONAL REFLECTION. All of us can think of times we were harmed by malicious taunts. Can you think of a time when you were harmed by words that were not aimed at you in particular?

The world is awash with bad words. The wise man and woman can spot them because they have characteristics that shrewd people can recognize. These proverbs reveal what bad words are like and how they do their damage. *Read the proverbs selected for this study.*

---

1. Evil communication can occur without a word being spoken. What are some of the ways this happens according to the proverbs you just read?

What other kinds of gestures do people use to communicate nonverbally?

---

2. Describe a time when you saw something like the nonverbal gestures mentioned in the proverbs above. What did you think when you saw them?

---

3. What kind of danger do you encounter when someone communicates something to you in this way?

4. Suppose you hear an inflammatory report about someone else. By hearing it, do you show yourself to be wicked or a liar (Proverbs 17:4)? Why or why not?

5. Imagine a plate of tasty morsels—elaborately decorated cookies, petit fours, canapés, hors d'oeuvres or something similar (Proverbs 18:8). What do those choice morsels have in common with the words of a gossip?

6. Do you think there's any danger in "innocently" overhearing the bad words that come from evil lips and malicious tongues? Explain.

7. Proverbs 26:23 points to a vulnerability we all face when listening to others' words: no matter how fervent they appear, they can, like a pottery glaze, hide something base underneath. Do you think there is any way to test words like you would evaluate a shiny piece of pottery?

8. Why does flattery threaten us in the same way that Proverbs 29:5 describes?

_____

9. Why is flattery simple to offer?

Why is flattery simple to accept?

_____

10. Thinking back over your previous answers, which is easier for you to produce—good words or bad words? Explain.

Avoiding the harm of bad words is impossible if we are a source of them ourselves. Pray as David did in Psalm 19:14:

> May the words of my mouth and the meditation of my heart
>   be pleasing in your sight, O LORD,
>   my Rock and my Redeemer.

Now or Later

Like smog, bad words are difficult to escape when they're "in the air" all around us. What can you do to reduce your exposure to such words in the coming weeks?

When words are many, sin is not absent,
    but he who holds his tongue is wise. (Proverbs 10:19)

A man finds joy in giving an apt reply—
    and how good is a timely word! (Proverbs 15:23)

Pleasant words are a honeycomb,
    sweet to the soul and healing to the bones. (Proverbs 16:24)

A rebuke impresses a man of discernment
    more than a hundred lashes a fool. (Proverbs 17:10)

An honest answer
    is like a kiss on the lips. (Proverbs 24:26)

A word aptly spoken
    is like apples of gold in settings of silver.

Like an earring of gold or an ornament of fine gold
    is a wise man's rebuke to a listening ear. (Proverbs 25:11-12)

6

Good Words

Speaking of the final judgment, Jesus said, "By your words you will be acquitted, and by your words you will be condemned" (Matthew 12:37). A similar idea is found in Proverbs 18:21:

> The tongue has the power of life and death,
>   and those who love it will eat its fruit.

Our words possess an awesome power for evil, but they also have an awesome power for good. For all that, words are not magic. Their power lies not so much in themselves as it does in the characters of those who speak them and those who hear them.

GROUP DISCUSSION. It is probably easy for you to think of times you heard words that caused harm. Think of a situation where someone's words were the cause of much good. Can you describe how those words produced that effect?

PERSONAL REFLECTION. Would you describe yourself as a person of few or many words? Explain.

Proverbs that speak about good words show them in action—especially from the perspective of those who receive them. *Read the proverbs selected for this study.*

1. As you look at the proverbs for this study, what characteristics do good words display?

2. Proverbs 10:19 suggests that the mere quantity of words produces sin. Why do you think that quantity alone is apt to produce sin in our own words?

3. Think about a situation where you are the most talkative. Why do you become so "wordy" in that situation?

4. What strategy might you employ to reduce or eliminate your wordiness? (Hint: don't forget the help that a friend or spouse can provide.)

5. Flattery is meant to be pleasant. Good words that are not flattery can also be pleasant. How can we distinguish flattery from the pleasant words Proverbs 16:24 and Proverbs 25:11-12 are talking about?

6. It's simple to understand how a deserved rebuke benefits a person with discernment (Proverbs 17:10). Imagine, however, that you receive an unjust or unfair rebuke. How might you still profit from it?

---

7. Take the previous situation one step further. How might onlookers benefit from observing how you profited from an unjust rebuke?

---

8. Ordinarily we exchange kisses on the lips only with special people in our lives. What characteristics distinguish these people from others we know?

---

9. Proverbs 24:26 compares an honest answer to a kiss on the lips. (Note: *honest* in Proverbs 24:26 has the sense of "straightforward" or "candid.") How are the answers and the kisses alike?

---

10. Proverbs 25:11-12 compares apt words with a piece of fine jewelry wrought in gold and silver. What characteristics do they have in common?

---

11. Think of someone you know whose speech is good. How does their speech demonstrate one or more of the proverbs listed in this study?

---

12. Good words, especially if they are going to have the quality of jewelry, will require some planning on your part. What can you do this week to prepare yourself to produce these kinds of words?

Our words are always producing fruit—for good or ill. Pray that you can learn to recognize wholesome speech, to reproduce its beauty in your own words and to enjoy the blessings that good words bestow.

Now or Later

Now that you have surveyed what the proverbs say about good and bad speech, which do you think is easier—to rid yourself of unwholesome speech habits or to build wholesome speech habits? Explain.

Go to the ant, you sluggard;
  consider its ways and be wise!

It has no commander,
  no overseer or ruler,

yet it stores its provisions in summer
  and gathers its food at harvest. (Proverbs 6:6-8)

The sluggard craves and gets nothing
  but the desires of the diligent are fully satisfied. (Proverbs 13:4)

The way of the sluggard is a hedge of thorns,
  but the path of the upright is a highway. (Proverbs 15:19)
  (author's translation)

The sluggard says, "There is a lion outside!"
  or, "I will be murdered in the streets!" (Proverbs 22:13)

I went past the field of the sluggard,
  past the vineyard of the man who lacks judgment;
thorns bad come up everywhere,
  the ground was covered with weeds,
  and the stone wall was in ruins.
I applied my heart to what I observed
  and learned a lesson from what I saw:
A little sleep, a little slumber,
  a little folding of the bands to rest—
and poverty will come on you like a bandit
  and scarcity like an armed man. (Proverbs 24:30-34)

As a door turns on its hinges,
  so a sluggard turns on his bed.

The sluggard buries his hand in the dish;
  he is too lazy to bring it back to his mouth.

The sluggard is wiser in his own eyes
  than seven men who answer discreetly. (Proverbs 26:14-16)

7

The Sluggard

Proverbs 6:6-8; 13:4; 15:19;
22:13; 24:30-34; 26:14-16

You've felt the urge before; you've heard the soft voice that says, "The messy garage will still be there tomorrow; the junky closet won't run away. Leave that weedy flower bed till the weekend. Wait a few more days for the rest of the bills to arrive, and then you can pay them all at once! If you wash the car now, it'll rain, and then where will you be? Rest up for tonight's party; you don't want to appear haggard. There's plenty of time to prepare the house after you're feeling refreshed." How often should we let the urge to catnap win out?

GROUP DISCUSSION. When you want to avoid an odious chore or an irksome project, what is your favorite excuse for doing so?

PERSONAL REFLECTION. What task are you most tempted to put off until later?

The proverbs on the sluggard are almost comic. Yet his prospects are bleak. Following Solomon's proverbs will save us from his fate. *Read the proverbs selected for this study.*

1. What are the characteristics of a sluggard that you find in this collection of proverbs?

2. Do you see any characteristics of a sluggard in these proverbs that surprise you? Explain.

3. Do you see a tendency in yourself that matches one of the sluggardly qualities mentioned in these proverbs?

4. In these proverbs, what character qualities are *contrasted* with sluggardliness?

5. Proverbs 15:19 shows us a surprising thing—a sluggard works *harder* than anyone else (that is, when he or she works at all). Why?

6. Describe one area of your life where a characteristic of a sluggard is evident (for example, housework, desk, various chores, yard work, grooming, wardrobe and so on). Be honest!

7. How does the example of the ant in Proverbs 6:6-8 highlight one remedy for sluggardliness?

8. How would you apply the remedy suggested by the ant to the one area of sluggardliness you mentioned previously?

9. Proverbs 24:30-34 ends with a vivid image describing the final condition of the sluggard—poverty. That poverty is compared to a thief and also to an armed man. What do you think is the point of this comparison? (What does poverty have in common with a thief? with an armed man?)

10. The proverbs hold out little hope for reforming a committed fool. On the other hand, why might there be some hope for reforming a sluggard?

---

11. Think once more of that task or project which brings out a sluggardly impulse in yourself. What can you do to avoid falling into the same old ways when that task comes round again?

To "just do it" is sometimes the hardest thing in the world! Even in a time of great personal need Jesus acknowledged that "the spirit is willing, but the body is weak" (Matthew 26:41). Pray to God to grant you the strength of will to be diligent in all your labors.

Now or Later

The sluggard's ability to come up with excuses is legendary (see Proverbs 22:13; 26:16). Do you think that making excuses is a symptom of sluggardliness or a cause of sluggardliness?

Lazy hands make a man poor,
  but diligent hands bring wealth. (Proverbs 10:4)

The wealth of the rich is their fortified city,
  but poverty is the ruin of the poor. (Proverbs 10:15)

The blessing of the LORD brings wealth,
  and he adds no trouble to it. (Proverbs 10:22)

A man's riches may ransom his life,
  but a poor man hears no threat. (Proverbs 13:8)

The wealth of the rich is their fortified city;
  they imagine it an unscalable wall. (Proverbs 18:11)

A poor man pleads for mercy,
  but a rich man answers harshly. (Proverbs 18:23)

Wealth brings many friends,
  but a poor man's friend deserts him. (Proverbs 19:4)

A fortune made by a lying tongue
  is a fleeting vapor and a deadly snare. (Proverbs 21:6)

Keep falsehood and lies far from me;
  give me neither poverty nor riches,
  but give me only my daily bread.
Otherwise, I may have too much and disown you
  and say, 'Who is the LORD?'
Or I may become poor and steal,
  and so dishonor the name of my God. (Proverbs 30:8-9)

8

Wealth & Poverty

When others are obviously rich or poor, we infer many things about their talents, education, personality, tastes and personal influence. But from the perspective of the proverbs, wealth and poverty are poor standards to use in judging others. Furthermore, Proverbs tells us it is foolish to suppose that wealth is an unmixed blessing and that poverty is always a curse.

GROUP DISCUSSION. Whether we think we're rich or poor often depends on our point of view. Who do you think of when you think of people richer than you? Who do you think of when you think of people who are poor? What would make you "feel" rich or poor? (Remember, we're thinking of *material* wealth and poverty.)

PERSONAL REFLECTION. Do you think you are rich or poor or neither? Why?

In a world that views wealth and poverty imperfectly, we need the precise, pithy standards in the proverbs to guide our steps away from snares that lie on every side. *Read the proverbs selected for this study.*

---

1. Some of the proverbs you read speak about several advantages of wealth. Are they the ones you would have thought of by yourself? Explain.

---

2. Looking over the same proverbs, what do you see to be some of the disadvantages of wealth?

---

3. Cite an example from your experience (or the experience of someone you know about) where an increase in wealth was a disadvantage.

---

4. Consider the first line of Proverbs 13:8: "A man's riches may ransom his life." How might that statement refer to either an advantage or a disadvantage of wealth?

---

5. After the second line of Proverbs 13:8 is considered, would you say the first line is speaking of an advantage or a disadvantage of wealth? Explain.

---

6. Proverbs 10:15 and 18:11 have the same first line. In each case, is the line expressing an advantage or disadvantage of wealth? Explain.

---

7. A recent tax statistic states that the top 10 percent of wage earners pay about 55 percent of the taxes collected each year. Are these facts consistent or inconsistent with statements in Proverbs? Why or why not?

---

8. Consider the disadvantages of poverty mentioned in the sampling of proverbs for this study. Do any of them surprise you? Why?

---

9. What advantages of poverty can you find in the proverbs for this study?

10. Can you think of a situation where your poverty (actual or perceived) proved to be an advantage to you?

---

11. It is easy to know if we're extravagantly rich or pitifully poor. But between these extremes the boundaries between poverty and wealth are hard to see. How does Proverbs 30:8-9 help us know when we are becoming perilously rich or poor?

The wise person seeks, among other things, to avoid extremes because they often present moral dangers. Pray, as the wise person does, to avoid extremes of poverty or wealth, so that neither will lead you into temptation.

Now or Later

To what extent have you embraced the attitude found in this petition in the Lord's Prayer: "Give me only my daily bread"? Explain.

He who despises his neighbor sins,
    but blessed is he who is kind to the needy. (Proverbs 14:21)

He who oppresses the poor shows contempt for their Maker,
    but whoever is kind to the needy honors God. (Proverbs 14:31)

Many curry favor with a ruler,
    and everyone is the friend of a man who gives gifts. (Proverbs 19:6)

He who is kind to the poor lends to the LORD,
    and he will reward him for what he has done. (Proverbs 19:17)

If a man shuts his ears to the cry of the poor,
    he too will cry out and not be answered. (Proverbs 21:13)

9

Giving

"The poor you have with you always," Jesus insisted on one occasion. And with the poor come knotty questions for all who view them with compassion: How can I meet so much need from my limited resources? How do I choose whom to help and whom to pass by? How do I balance the needs of the poor with the requests for help from my children, my aged parents or my extended family?

GROUP DISCUSSION. Think of the appeals for help that come to you in the mail, on television, in your churches; they frequently show you people in dire physical need. What do you think when you see these kinds of appeals?

PERSONAL REFLECTION. What makes you immediately dismiss an appeal for help?

The proverbs in this study can guide us through the moral conflicts we encounter when confronted with the material neediness of others. Additionally, they give an antidote to the folly which exalts acquisitiveness as a social and economic virtue. Our prosperity, it turns out, may be a result of our giving rather than our getting! *Read the proverbs selected for this study.*

1. Is Proverbs 14:21 referring to all the needy in the world, or is a narrower group in view? Explain.

2. What needy people do you know who fall into that category?

3. A translation that preserves the ambiguity in the Hebrew original of 14:31 reads, "He who oppresses the poor shows contempt for his maker, but whoever is kind to the needy honors him." Whose Maker is shown contempt by oppression—the poor man's Maker or the oppressor's Maker? Explain.

4. Whose Maker is honored by kindness to the needy—the needy person's Maker or the kind person's Maker?

5. If you are generous, and consequently might attract a lot of "friends," how can you avoid the problem described in Proverbs 19:6?

6. Do you think that the "friends" who flock around a generous giver are always a problem? Why or why not?

7. Proverbs 19:17 implies a motive for giving that is almost never mentioned or, if mentioned, viewed as sub-Christian. What is it?

8. Why do you think people are uncomfortable with that kind of motive for giving implied in Proverbs 19:17?

9. Suppose the mail carrier brings you a request for money to feed hungry orphans in some far-off land and you throw this appeal into the wastepaper basket. Is your action going to call down on yourself the calamity Proverbs 21:13 speaks about? Explain.

10. Beginning this week, how can your giving to the poor reflect the wisdom of these proverbs?

Ask God to grow compassion in you.

Now or Later

How does your benevolence to the poor show honor to God?

The integrity of the upright guides them,
    but the unfaithful are destroyed by their duplicity. (Proverbs 11:3)

There is a way that seems right to a man,
    but in the end it leads to death. (Proverbs 14:12)

Plans fail for lack of counsel,
    but with many advisers they succeed. (Proverbs 15:22)

In his heart a man plans his course,
    but the LORD determines his steps. (Proverbs 16:9)

The plans of the diligent lead to profit
    as surely as haste leads to poverty. (Proverbs 21:5)

The horse is made ready for the day of battle,
    but victory rests with the LORD. (Proverbs 21:31)

Do not boast about tomorrow,
    for you do not know what a day may bring forth. (Proverbs 27:1)

10

Planning the Future

Proverbs 11:3; 14:12; 15:22;
16:9; 21:5, 31; 27:1

No doubt you've glanced once or twice at an astrologer's predictions in the newspaper. Even if you felt guilty or silly for doing it, you'd hardly fault yourself for wanting every possible advantage in planning your future. Planning for the future, after all, is a major industry. Hundreds of billions of dollars ride on the forecasts of economists, investment counselors, analysts of every sort and even astrologers! Legions of advisers will sell you opinions on what will happen in the near term and long term. Whether or not you take their advice, someone else will. And in turn that person's actions may affect your prosperity, health and happiness.

GROUP DISCUSSION. What kinds of things in the future do you find it good to plan for?

PERSONAL REFLECTION. Do you ever feel that planning for the future is pointless? Why?

For all their focus on the here and now, the proverbs keep a canny eye on the future. Many proverbs, in fact, offer wisdom on how to make plans. They tell us why we should plan for the future and what we can expect of the best plans we make. *Read over the proverbs selected for this study.*

1. Based on these proverbs, why might your plans for the future go awry?

2. When has one of your plans failed for one of the reasons mentioned in these proverbs?

3. What character qualities mentioned in these proverbs make it hard to plan for the future?

4. We usually evaluate a plan according to its merits, not on the basis of the character of the planner. Why does a planner's character make a difference?

5. Proverbs 15:22 specifies many counselors. What do many counselors provide over a few or even one counselor?

6. Proverbs 21:5 says that a good plan by itself is not enough to yield success. What part does diligence play?

7. An atheist could profitably apply what we've seen in these studies. Yet how do the proverbs in this study also point to a divine dimension in the plans we make (and, indeed, in all wisdom)?

_____

8. How would your planning differ from an atheist's?

_____

9. Do Proverbs 16:9 and 21:31 encourage or discourage careful planning? Explain.

_____

10. Do you think that wise plans invariably succeed? Why or why not?

_____

11. What is something in your future which you have not planned for at all? What can you begin to do to make plans?

Now or Later
Does Proverbs 27:1 argue against making plans for the future? Why or why not?

Leader's Notes

Leading a Bible discussion can be an enjoyable and rewarding experience. But it can also be *scary*—especially if you've never done it before. If this is your feeling, you're in good company. When God asked Moses to lead the Israelites out of Egypt, he replied, "O Lord, please send someone else to do it"! (Ex 4:13). It was the same with Solomon, Jeremiah and Timothy, but God helped these people in spite of their weaknesses, and he will help you as well.

You don't need to be an expert on the Bible or a trained teacher to lead a Bible discussion. The idea behind these inductive studies is that the leader guides group members to discover for themselves what the Bible has to say. This method of learning will allow group members to remember much more of what is said than a lecture would.

These studies are designed to be led easily. As a matter of fact, the flow of questions through the passage from observation to interpretation to application is so natural that you may feel that the studies lead themselves. This study guide is also flexible. You can use it with a variety of groups—student, professional, neighborhood or church groups. Each study takes forty-five to sixty minutes in a group setting.

There are some important facts to know about group dynamics and encouraging discussion. The suggestions listed below should enable you to effectively and enjoyably fulfill your role as leader.

Preparing for the Study

1. Ask God to help you understand and apply the passage in your

own life. Unless this happens, you will not be prepared to lead others. Pray too for the various members of the group. Ask God to open your hearts to the message of his Word and motivate you to action.

2. Read the introduction to the entire guide to get an overview of the entire book and the issues which will be explored.

3. As you begin each study, read and reread the assigned Bible passage to familiarize yourself with it.

4. This study guide is based on the New International Version of the Bible. It will help you and the group if you use this translation as the basis for your study and discussion.

5. Carefully work through each question in the study. Spend time in meditation and reflection as you consider how to respond.

6. Write your thoughts and responses in the space provided in the study guide. This will help you to express your understanding of the passage clearly.

7. It might help to have a Bible dictionary handy. Use it to look up any unfamiliar words, names or places. (For additional help on how to study a passage, see chapter five of *How to Lead a LifeGuide Bible Study*, IVP.)

8. Consider how you can apply the Scripture to your life. Remember that the group will follow your lead in responding to the studies. They will not go any deeper than you do.

9. Once you have finished your own study of the passage, familiarize yourself with the leader's notes for the study you are leading. These are designed to help you in several ways. First, they tell you the purpose the study guide author had in mind when writing the study. Take time to think through how the study questions work together to accomplish that purpose. Second, the notes provide you with additional background information or suggestions on group dynamics for various questions. This information can be useful when people have difficulty understanding or answering a question. Third, the leader's notes can alert you to potential problems you may encounter during the study.

10. If you wish to remind yourself of anything mentioned in the leader's notes, make a note to yourself below that question in the study.

Leading the Study

1. Begin the study on time. Open with prayer, asking God to help the group to understand and apply the passage.

2. Be sure that everyone in your group has a study guide. Encourage the group to prepare beforehand for each discussion by reading the introduction to the guide and by working through the questions in the study.

3. At the beginning of your first time together, explain that these studies are meant to be discussions, not lectures. Encourage the members of the group to participate. However, do not put pressure on those who may be hesitant to speak during the first few sessions. You may want to suggest the following guidelines to your group.

☐ Stick to the topic being discussed.

☐ Your responses should be based on the verses which are the focus of the discussion and not on outside authorities such as commentaries or speakers.

☐ These studies focus on a particular passage of Scripture. Only rarely should you refer to other portions of the Bible. This allows for everyone to participate in in-depth study on equal ground.

☐ Anything said in the group is considered confidential and will not be discussed outside the group unless specific permission is given to do so.

☐ We will listen attentively to each other and provide time for each person present to talk.

☐ We will pray for each other.

4. Have a group member read the introduction at the beginning of the discussion.

5. Every session begins with a group discussion question. The question or activity is meant to be used before the passage is read. The question introduces the theme of the study and encourages group members to begin to open up. Encourage as many members as possible to participate, and be ready to get the discussion going with your own response.

This section is designed to reveal where our thoughts or feelings need to be transformed by Scripture. That is why it is especially important not to read the passage before the discussion question is asked. The passage will tend to color the honest reactions people would otherwise give because they are, of course, supposed to think the way the Bible does.

You may want to supplement the group discussion question with an icebreaker to help people to get comfortable. See the community section of *Small Group Idea Book* for more ideas.

You also might want to use the personal reflection question with your group. Either allow a time of silence for people to respond individually or discuss it together.

6. Have a group member (or members if the passage is long) read aloud the passage to be studied. Then give people several minutes to read the passage again silently so that they can take it all in.

7. Question 1 will generally be an overview question designed to briefly survey the passage. Encourage the group to look at the whole passage, but try to avoid getting sidetracked by questions or issues that will be addressed later in the study.

8. As you ask the questions, keep in mind that they are designed to be used just as they are written. You may simply read them aloud. Or you may prefer to express them in your own words.

There may be times when it is appropriate to deviate from the study guide. For example, a question may have already been answered. If so, move on to the next question. Or someone may raise an important question not covered in the guide. Take time to discuss it, but try to keep the group from going off on tangents.

9. Avoid answering your own questions. If necessary, repeat or rephrase them until they are clearly understood. Or point out something you read in the leader's notes to clarify the context or meaning. An eager group quickly becomes passive and silent if they think the leader will do most of the talking.

10. Don't be afraid of silence. People may need time to think about the question before formulating their answers.

11. Don't be content with just one answer. Ask, "What do the rest of you think?" or "Anything else?" until several people have given answers to the question.

12. Acknowledge all contributions. Try to be affirming whenever possible. Never reject an answer. If it is clearly off-base, ask, "Which

verse led you to that conclusion?" or again, "What do the rest of you think?"

13. Don't expect every answer to be addressed to you, even though this will probably happen at first. As group members become more at ease, they will begin to truly interact with each other. This is one sign of healthy discussion.

14. Don't be afraid of controversy. It can be very stimulating. If you don't resolve an issue completely, don't be frustrated. Move on and keep it in mind for later. A subsequent study may solve the problem.

15. Periodically summarize what the group has said about the passage. This helps to draw together the various ideas mentioned and gives continuity to the study. But don't preach.

16. At the end of the Bible discussion you may want to allow group members a time of quiet to work on an idea under "Now or Later." Then discuss what you experienced. Or you may want to encourage group members to work on these ideas between meetings. Give an opportunity during the session for people to talk about what they are learning.

17. Conclude your time together with conversational prayer, adapting the prayer suggestion at the end of the study to your group. Ask for God's help in following through on the commitments you've made.

18. End on time.

Many more suggestions and helps are found in *How to Lead a LifeGuide Bible Study*.

Components of Small Groups

A healthy small group should do more than study the Bible. There are four components to consider as you structure your time together.

Nurture. Small groups help us to grow in our knowledge and love of God. Bible study is the key to making this happen and is the foundation of your small group.

Community. Small groups are a great place to develop deep friendships with other Christians. Allow time for informal interaction before and after each study. Plan activities and games that will help you get to know each other. Spend time having fun together—going on a picnic or cooking dinner together.

Worship and prayer. Your study will be enhanced by spending time praising God together in prayer or song. Pray for each other's needs—and keep track of how God is answering prayer in your group. Ask God to help you to apply what you are learning in your study.

Outreach. Reaching out to others can be a practical way of applying what you are learning, and it will keep your group from becoming self-focused. Host a series of evangelistic discussions for your friends or neighbors. Clean up the yard of an elderly friend. Serve at a soup kitchen together, or spend a day working on a Habitat house.

Many more suggestions and helps in each of these areas are found in *Small Group Idea Book.* Information on building a small group can be found in *Small Group Leaders' Handbook* and *The Big Book on Small Groups* (both from InterVarsity Press). Reading through one of these books would be worth your time.

Study 1. Proverbs 9. The Choice.

Purpose: To hear and accept Lady Wisdom's invitation to become wise.

Question 1. Lady Wisdom's feast appears quite lavish, not only in its venue (possibly a palace setting), but also in its menu. Woman Folly's feast is hardly a feast—the only things mentioned are bread and water!

Question 2. It's interesting that Lady Wisdom's and Woman Folly's invitations mirror one another at one point—the persons specifically addressed in the invitations. Note that verses 4 and 16 are identical.

Question 3. Obviously if you think you're invited then you agree that you're one of the simple. Many lack the personal humility to admit this about themselves. Draw people out concerning a specific area where they think they're "simple," where they know that they don't have good judgment. If someone honestly insists that he or she doesn't need to accept Lady Wisdom's invitation, don't press them to change their mind. Tactfully move the discussion to someone else in the group. (For why you should do this, read Proverbs 9:12-17.)

Question 4. Certainly no one would invite people to a feast if those invited were going to act rudely or hatefully toward the host or hostess! But this is exactly the kind of response that Lady Wisdom says a mocker will give to someone who tries to correct them. There is no way Lady Wisdom will invite these kinds of people into her home.

Question 5. Clearly Lady Wisdom has vast resources—her maids and the seven-pillared house suggest substantial wealth, as does her menu. By contrast, Woman Folly must sit outside her house or travel to the crossroads of the city to make herself heard.

Question 6. The answer here depends entirely on what one means by pleasure. Certainly Woman Folly promises that the stolen water will be sweet and the secretly eaten bread will be delicious. There's a warning, however, in that she implies that the water is sweet because it is stolen. The pleasures she offers, therefore, are illicit. By contrast, Lady Wisdom makes no explicit promise of pleasure in these verses (for these, see passages such as Prov 3:13-26 and 4:8-13), but she does offer long life and the rewards that wisdom brings (9:11-12).

Question 7. The verbs of these verses give the answer—to correct, to rebuke, to instruct, to teach. Lady Wisdom's fare is hardly pablum!

Question 8. When speaking of truth, wisdom, ethics or anything else claiming to make affirmations about ultimate reality, some suppose that "religious" truth is somehow different from "secular" truth, and that only "religious" truth is in view in Proverbs 9:10. However, a quick survey of the contents of Proverbs reveals that the proverbs deal with nonreligious matters as often as religious ones. It's trite to repeat, perhaps, but "all truth is God's truth." For this reason, all truth proceeds from and leads to a knowledge of God himself.

Does this mean that knowledge must be explicitly Judeo-Christian to be authentic? No, for there's strong evidence that many of the proverbs in the book of Proverbs arose in non-Jewish cultures. And where, for example, are the explicit Judeo-Christian features of the Pythagorean theorem?

On the other hand, Proverbs, its larger Old Testament context and later Christian revelation all unite in affirming that truth is essentially a viewpoint, that it is finally the viewpoint of One who is Truth itself, or rather Truth himself. Accordingly, all knowledge is knowledge about God, if only dimly perceived (or unperceived) by an individual knower. And the straightest way toward wisdom is to fear the God whose wisdom it is.

Question 9. Strive for two things in discussing this question: (1) to multiply examples of "Lady Wisdoms" in everyone's life, and (2) to specify precisely how the persons mentioned accomplish for each of us what Lady Wisdom is said to accomplish.

Lady Wisdom appears in anyone (male or female) who relates to us as a reprover, corrector, instructor, protector, benefactor or patron. Parents are obvious examples. So are teachers of every kind. To these we can add physicians, dentists and other doctors; athletic coaches and other trainers; lifeguards at the beach; auto mechanics who warn us about our slack engine maintenance; a store clerk knowledgeable in some product or service we wish to buy; any neighbor, friend, coworker or family member experienced in things where we are not experienced.

Question 10. Again, during the discussion endeavor to concretize as much as possible situations or circumstances where Woman Folly is encountered in everyday living (in people who may be male as often as female). Examples include all those who entice us with the promise of pleasure or profit from illicit activities. Much advertising comes from Woman Folly as well.

Questions 11-12. The fun from Woman Folly's feast comes, as said before, from the illicit pleasures of forbidden indulgence. The pain is protracted as long as death itself. In Lady Wisdom one meets the pain that invariably attends reproof. But such pain is as fleeting as Woman Folly's pleasure, while the rewards are a long life to enjoy the fruits of wisdom. It may seem selfish, but our own well-being is the fundamental reason for choosing wisdom.

Study 2. Proverbs 7. The Simple.
Purpose: To recognize the simpleton in ourselves by developing a simpleton's profile from selected proverbs.

Question 1. Verses 1-5 and 24-27 are a father's words to his son, exhorting him to avoid folly by giving him warnings about what will happen if the son is seduced by foolishness. As a concrete example of what he is talking about, the father relates a scene he has actually observed. There is no reason to doubt that what Solomon describes in these verses is something he actually witnessed from his own palace, which overlooked the streets of Jerusalem.

Question 2. The scene takes place at dusk. A young man, seemingly at loose ends, meets a woman with definite designs on fulfilling her own lusts.

Question 3. Evidently the young man is "unconnected." There seems to be no one around to see him dally with the forward woman—no family, no parents, no friends. The falling darkness probably gives him further ideas of being able to get away with something unseen.

Question 4. Probably true: she has food at home after fulfilling her vows at the temple; she's made preparations to receive a lover; her husband is gone on a trip and is expected to remain a long time. Probably false: she's been looking just for him; they can indulge their lusts without danger of discovery or unhappy consequences.

Question 5. Good examples may be found in all sorts of petty crimes and misdemeanors—drugs, vandalism, theft and so on.

Question 6. Of course on the page it will probably appear overly dramatic. But to disprove this all one needs to do is consider the crimes of sexual passion that are routinely reported in the evening television news. Assault, murder and mayhem are not uncommon consequences of what we read about in Proverbs 7. And, of course, the same may be said for many other kinds of folly.

Question 7. The young man believes the woman because he is too naive to see through her cheap flattery. He never considers the consequences of taking her invitation, so he is wholly unprepared for the trouble that will sooner or later befall him.

Question 8. An area of "simpleness" might include negotiating a real estate deal, investing $100,000 from an inheritance, organizing an evangelistic coffee time in a home, planting a vegetable garden, buying an automobile. Help draw out responses by suggesting categories—personal relationships, jobs, money management, recreation and so on. Be ready to offer a number of areas which are not explicitly spiritual so that simpleness is seen to include more than the "religious."

Question 10. Prudence is acquired through knowledge and experience no matter what the area of living. Turn the discussion toward specific activities that will educate and give experience in the area where prudence is sought.

Study 3. Proverbs 13:19; 17:12; 18:2, 7; 20:3; 26:11. Avoiding the Fool.

Purpose: To develop the habit of "defensive living" by avoiding dangerous folly we encounter daily.

General note. Several problems enter into group discussions of the fool. Many will be reluctant to identify others as fools or admit to manifestations of foolishness in themselves, making it difficult to discuss specific situations. Someone may even quote Jesus in Matthew 5:22: "But anyone who says, 'You fool!' will be in danger of the fire of hell."

Several strategies meet these problems. You can encourage the group from the beginning to avoid referring to people (other than themselves) by name. Often current events will supply public figures whose foolish actions serve as incarnations of these proverbs. Fictional characters familiar to all in the group are another source. Explain that Jesus didn't prohibit the application of the label fool to one who has earned it; rather he warns against an angry, scornful attitude which is comparable to murder.

Question 1. A bear robbed of her cubs is an obvious danger, while fools may not seem dangerous when we first meet them. Within broad limits one knows what to expect of a bear robbed of her cubs and what to do to avoid her dangers. In the case of fools, we might not step away in time to avoid the calamity their folly brings.

Question 3. The strong implication from Proverbs 18:2 is that the fool's opinions are riddled with misunderstanding. Insofar as fools insist on airing those opinions they display ignorance to those who know better. When fools act on their own opinions they reap the consequences.

Question 4. Someone who is always talking, especially if their talking seems never to take into account what others are saying, makes the fool's own mouth a great "fool detector."

Question 5. At the heart of a fool is an obsessive self-esteem. They think so highly of themselves that others' opinions cannot have any merit. Consequently they are always talking, never listening. This behavior is exactly opposite to how a wise person acts.

Question 6. If the second line begins with *so*, then it implies that evil is something the fool longs for and therefore does not turn away from.

"The proverb shows us that a fool's problem is not a mental or educational deficiency; rather he is morally bent toward wickedness." See further A. Cohen, *Proverbs* (Brooklyn, N.Y.: Soncino, 1946); Franz Delitzsh and C. F. Keil, *Proverbs, Ecclesiastes, Song of Solomon* (Grand Rapids, Mich.: Eerdmans, 1971).

Question 7. Without differences of viewpoint or agenda there can be no quarrel. The fool's quickness to quarrel arises from two factors—his contrariness to all that is sound, sane and sensible in the world around him, and his settled conviction that he is right and everyone else is wrong.

Question 8. A great variety of insightful observations are possible. Be sure, however, to highlight two: (1) This is "natural" for a dog. This is the kind of thing dogs do because they are dogs. Thus this image speaks to the incorrigibility of a fool's character. (2) The image is revolting. If we can contemplate such behavior in a dog without disgust, this says something unsavory about us. How much more if a fool fails to awaken revulsion in us.

Question 9. If possible, encourage competing views to surface so that you can interact. Clearly the proverbs encourage us to assess another's character and possibly render a verdict that he or she is a fool. Jesus warns us that the same evaluations we apply to others can be—or will be—applied to us (Mt 7:2-5). But this cannot mean that we abstain from making these judgments altogether. The proverbs warn us that failing to recognize and avoid the fool will be hazardous to our own character, well-being, even our lives. A glance at Matthew 7:6 shows that Jesus agrees.

Question 10. If you feel you are comfortable enough as a group, you might ask people to cite how their behavior is foolish. Or you can make the first part of the question silent reflection and just talk about your goals for change.

Study 4. Proverbs 13:10, 20; 14:12; 15:12; 21:30; 25:12. Finding Wisdom.

Purpose: To equip ourselves to seek out skills we lack from wise men and women who have those skills.

Question 1. Two proverbs have experience in view. Proverbs 13:20 recommends walking with the wise, that is, sharing their experience.

Proverbs 14:12 indicates the possibility of learning better than we originally thought, assuming that we survive the mistakes in judgment we make.

In general, however, the proverbs indicate that wisdom is something best received from wise people rather than from raw experience. Whether or not wisdom comes through advice (Prov 13:10), correction (Prov 15:12) or rebuke (Prov 25:12), wisdom is best imparted from wise people to those who would be wise.

Question 2. Whether we learn by raw experience alone or through the mentoring of a wise man or woman, it is invariable that we must face our own faults and flaws. If our character cannot receive correction, we cannot become wise.

Question 4. Many ideas are possible of course. A good school would have some of the following features: (1) a well-defined curriculum emphasizing specific concepts or techniques rather than one that leaves the student to develop on his own (Prov 13:10); (2) teachers accomplished and successful in their subject area (Prov 13:20); (3) a teaching philosophy that seeks to correct unwise behavior (Prov 15:12); (4) values and goals that are not contrary to God's (Prov 21:30); (5) graduates who esteem the school for what it accomplished in them (Prov 25:12).

Question 6. Inexpensive and ready sources of wisdom exist among one's acquaintances. All around us are people with skills valuable to us. If approached properly, their skills may become our skills. Offering to help them is one way to learn from them. Sometimes simply asking their advice will open up a learning dimension to your relationship with them.

Question 7. "Wising up" means confronting our faults, flaws and weaknesses. Many times it will be unpleasant to learn about these, especially if we thought they were our strengths! To become wise we must be able and willing to change our mind about ourselves. This is not always easy or pleasant.

Question 9. It's always what we don't know that gets us. Human knowledge is limited, and decisions based on our own, solitary understanding cannot help but be riddled with inaccuracy.

Question 10. The simplest answer is that we can't know for certain.

Proverbs 21:30 reminds us that when God is at work in history, his agenda will overrule any competing ones, even if they are otherwise "righteous" (that is, not involving actual transgression). The best we can do (and should do) is to test whether our goals and means to achieve them are in harmony with God's character and purposes revealed in Scripture.

Study 5. Proverbs 6:12-14; 16:30; 17:4; 18:8; 26:23; 29:5. Bad Words.

Purpose: To inoculate ourselves against the harmful consequences of foolish or evil speech.

Question 1. Role playing these proverbs can generate some immediate and pungent insights. If possible, let three people play-act a scene not more than 15-20 seconds long. The cast of characters should include an evil, silent communicator, the one to whom he or she directs the silent speech and the one about whom he or she communicates. The latter character is a victim, a target, an object of derision, scorn or attack. Because the "speaker" is present in the same room as the victim, the former character must resort to gestures to make his or her point about the victim without the victim's knowing it.

Question 3. It is dangerous to hear this kind of speech, for it makes the "hearer" a collaborator. To receive such communication not only makes us look, it also makes us join and then share the hostility, if only for a moment, against the victim. After the first step of "listening," it may be awkward or difficult to retreat, and the temptation to explore further what the pointer means may prove irresistible.

Question 4. Of course, bad words are not magical; they have no power to transform your character as soon as you hear them. The verbs "listen to" and "pay attention to" suggest that when the hearer "has an ear" for this kind of thing, it is correct to characterize such a person as wicked or a liar.

Question 5. If possible, create a master list that everyone can see at once on a blackboard, a large paper tablet or an overhead projector. It's fun to go around the group, letting one person after another contribute an observation, until everyone's suggestions are exhausted.

The master list then becomes the common point of discussion about this proverb. The point not to miss is this: the attractiveness of gossip; its desirability; its power to please, to whet an appetite, to develop a taste for itself in its hearers.

Question 6. Once consumed, such gossip is nearly impossible to dislodge. Even if we think it malicious, false or destructive, it remains with us as something to cope with.

Question 7. If the group has difficulty understanding this proverb, point out that fervent lips are compared to an attractive coating of glaze, and an evil heart is compared to worthless earthenware. The obvious threat that Proverbs 26:23 points out is this: that by their artfulness, their beauty or their sparkle (some obvious features of glaze on pottery) bad words may mask a base and worthless character (corresponding to the worthless clay beneath the glaze). A second threat—words have great power to deceive, and if this fact hardens a listener's ear with cynicism, he or she may not only reject the evil that words can do but also the great good that wholesome, truthful words can bring.

Protection? Those knowledgeable about ceramics can spot the cheap ones, even if they have pretty glaze. To spot the evil heart covered with fervent lips requires a similar discernment about people.

Question 8. Answers to this question may or may not be helpful, depending on the number of genuinely humble people in the group. It takes authentic humility to admit giving or receiving flattery, especially flattery which leads to harm. Be prepared with your own example and draw the discussion around it if necessary.

Question 9. In a word, giving or receiving flattery is *easy*. The alternatives to flattery (silence or some very skillful and diplomatic truth telling) is usually difficult. Most of us would rather say something nice than something critical, yet we sometimes lack skill to discern something authentically good to comment on. Add to this our potential profit from pleasing another, and you have a powerful inducement to flattery. As for *hearing* flattery, who can honestly say that they prefer criticism?

Study 6. Proverbs 10:19; 15:23; 16:24; 17:10; 24:26; 25:11-12. Good Words.

Purpose: To acquire the ability to do good through our words by developing wholesome habits of speech.

Question 1. The qualities of good words are almost sensual according to these proverbs. They are beautiful, sweet, wholesome and healing. Though only one proverb actually makes the comparison to food (Prov 16:24), we get the sense from these proverbs that good words are like delicious, healthy food.

Question 2. In the previous study, we saw how easy it is to speak bad words, while speaking good ones requires considerable practice and effort. Consequently, the more we speak, the more opportunity there is for error and harm.

Question 4. As far as words are concerned, the fundamental difference between a wise man or woman and a foolish one is this: folly speaks easily and generously; wisdom is slow to speak and quick to listen, which involves no speaking at all. Therefore the primary tactic to overcome wordiness is simply to refrain from speaking at all! To make this socially possible, one might strive to develop a habit of querying others to draw them out, while refraining from offering one's own comments until and unless they are requested. Specific strategies might enlist the help of a friend or spouse (who can tap us under the table).

Question 5. For a fool or a simpleton, it will be very difficult to tell the difference, as he or she may enjoy hearing either. Healing implies some harm or deficiency in ourselves that the pleasant words make better. If we're humble enough to recognize a defect in ourselves, we'll be able to distinguish words that improve our faults from words which merely gloss them over.

Question 6. Even if we were unjustly or incorrectly rebuked, the rebuke itself alerts us to the perceptions of the one who delivers the rebuke. Far more important than defending ourselves would be to seek out what prompted the rebuker to criticize us in the first place.

Question 7. Our modeling of wisdom can help wisdom grow in those with eyes to watch.

Questions 8-9. The point of this proverb stands out once we ask if a kiss on the lips from a total stranger is different from a kiss on the lips from a special person. One we'll gladly accept; the other we'll reject as an outlandish intrusion, even if skillfully delivered. No matter how wholesome or profitable a candid answer may be to us, we receive them like we receive kisses—from those we esteem, our confidants, our lovers, our intimate friends. The proverb says a lot about those to whom we offer our candid observations. Other than the erotic contexts of the Song of Songs, this is the only reference in the Old Testament to kissing the lips.

Question 10. Among the characteristics of apt words are their great value, their striking beauty, and the obvious artistry involved in their execution. To speak apt words, we need the skills (and the practice) required to produce them, even as a jeweler must spend considerable time developing skills to fashion precious metals into works of art.

Study 7. Proverbs 6:6-8; 13:4; 15:19; 22:13; 24:30-34; 26:14-16. The Sluggard.

Purpose: To avoid the fate of the sluggard by noting how his laziness frustrates everything in his life.

Question 1. The following characteristics are the more obvious ones, though others are possible depending on the nuances detected in a proverb: never finishes things (Prov 26:15), fond of sleep (Prov 24:30-34; 26:14), rationalizes (Prov 22:13), believes his own excuses (Prov 26:16), never starts things (Prov 22:1, 3; 26:14, by implication), never satisfied (Prov 13:14).

Question 3. Use this question to encourage everyone to loosen up a bit about their own faults here.

Question 4. Characteristics include self-directing (Prov 6:6-8), diligence (Prov 13:4), uprightness (Prov 15:19), wisdom (Prov 26:16). Of course, simple meditation on an ant's ways will suggest other characteristics, the most obvious ones being diligence, persistence and teamwork.

Question 5. Proverbs 15:19 says the sluggard's way is a hedge of thorns; that is, his movement is fraught with hindrances and difficulties. By contrast, the path of the upright is smooth and easy. The ironic point is that lazy people, when they work at all, must work harder and with greater difficulties than the upright! By avoiding work, they avoid *efficient* work. So when necessity forces them to work, they find their work to be difficult and inefficient.

Question 7. If one characteristic stands out in the ant, it is persistence. The work that any one ant does at any time is small in relation to the overall task. But the job gets done because every ant does its part faithfully. Hard work might, after all, come from sloth. Persistent work is a virtue.

Question 8. The point to highlight here is to break projects into manageable segments rather than letting them grow so large through neglect that they must be done in a single Herculean effort. Make the point by letting the group brainstorm a plan of action for one or two areas of sluggardliness that were mentioned earlier.

Question 9. The poverty which overcomes the sluggard is like a thief in that it sneaks up unawares. Its onset is not sudden or shocking. We can see that the sluggard grows poor in stages that match his own slowness to work. There is nothing the sluggard can do to ward off poverty, as it came about with a long investment of laziness which cannot be counterbalanced by feverish, sudden activity.

Question 10. If there's any hope for the sluggard, it is in realizing that avoiding work only postpones a problem. Doing work eliminates the problem. And of course the rewards for the latter replace the penalties of the former. Said another way, the man or woman who really wants to work less will work smarter, not harder.

Study 8. Proverbs 10:4, 15, 22; 13:8; 18:11, 23; 19:4; 21:6; 30:8-9. Wealth & Poverty.
Purpose: To reevaluate the standards we use when we assess the advantages and disadvantages of material possessions.

Questions 1-2. Advantages of wealth: protection and security, as a fortified city provides protection and security (10:15); the ability to ransom life (13:8); many friends (19:4). Be aware that group members may confuse the advantages or disadvantages of wealth with things that result in wealth. Someone, for example, may suggest that wealth shows that one is in favor with God (Prov 10:22) or conversely that wealth shows that someone is dishonest (Prov 21:6).

Disadvantages of wealth: it can deceive the wealthy person (Prov 18:11); it can foster harshness in the wealthy person (Prov 18:23); it can develop an arrogant independence from God (Prov 30:8-9).

Celebrity figures will furnish multiple examples. Many such personalities show clearly that increasing one's options and one's ability to choose them is a curse for the man or woman whose character tends toward sin or folly.

Questions 4. Wealth is a disadvantage insofar as it becomes a pretext for holding a wealthy man's life ransom (for example, poor people don't attract kidnappers seeking monetary ransoms). This idea reads ransom in a concrete sense. If we read ransom in a more figurative sense—that wealth is like a ransom for one's life—then the proverb claims that wealth has power to preserve or prolong life, as when wealthy people can afford expensive, lifesaving medical care or even a more healthful diet than those who are utterly impoverished.

Question 5. As the proverb seems to be contrasting two ideas, the absence of a threat for the poor would suggest the presence of a threat for the rich—hence that Proverbs 13:8 is speaking of a disadvantage of wealth.

Question 6. The first line of Proverbs 10:15 expresses an advantage of wealth, which is contrasted with a corresponding disadvantage of poverty in the second line. In Proverbs 18:11, however, the sense of the first line is more ironic. While not denying the security of wealth, that security may be more imaginary than real and thus more a liability than an asset.

Question 7. A popular myth says that rich people have options available to them to avoid taxation that people of lesser incomes do not have. Like all really good myths this one has a few roots in reality, mostly in the fact that wealth brings not only more options for investment and acquisition but also exposes one to a greater variety of taxation (and corresponding strategies to reduce taxation). Governments take money from those who have it. Dallas economist Scott Burns said it succinctly: "The rich are different; they pay more taxes" (*Dallas Morning News*, December 27, 1988, business section, p. 1).

Questions 8-9. Disadvantages of poverty: poverty can lead to ruin beyond poverty (Prov 10:15); poverty can reduce a man to utter dependence on another for mercy (18:23); poverty diminishes the circle of one's friends (Prov 19:24); poverty can lead to sin (Prov 30:8-9). Advantages of poverty: the poor are free from threats that wealth attracts (Prov 13:8); the poor avoid the deceptions of wealth (Prov 18:11); the poor escape the character corruption that can result from wealth (Prov 18:23).

Question 10. Difficulty in naming examples may arise because most examples are negative—that is, they consist of things that did not happen because of actual or perceived poverty. A trivial but actual case: those who drive "junker" automobiles almost never suffer auto theft or theft of property from their vehicles.

Question 11. We become too rich when we are tempted to depend on our wealth more than God. We become too poor at the point where our poverty tempts us to transgress God's law. Wealth or poverty tests one's character and reveals what it really is.

Study 9. Proverbs 14:21, 31; 19:6, 17; 21:13. Giving.
Purpose: To discern how best to help others through giving.
General note. When a group discusses giving, some will often expand the notion of giving to include giving of time, talent, friendship and affirmation, or the poor will be made to include those who are "poor" in education, opportunities, appearance, friends and so on. The proverbs and most texts in the Bible about giving envision the poor to be those impoverished in material needs, such as food, clothing or shelter. To give is to supply those material needs out of one's own material resources. While it is often useful to extrapolate the teaching of the proverbs from their immediate sense to related areas, such extrapolation is best done after the proverbs have been understood in concrete terms. How can we talk of giving things like affirmation or friendship if we've not teamed to give away the extra coat in the closet?

Question 1. The needy in Proverbs 14:21 are our needy neighbors, as a comparison of the lines indicates. They are the needy we meet in our neighborhood, among our friends—the ones we see as we move about our routine paths in our schools, workplaces and churches. Proverbs 14:21 directs our attention to those needy immediately in our presence, whom we can often help immediately.

Questions 3-4. God may be shown contempt when his creatures are oppressed, just as any artist is shown contempt when his artwork is defamed, derided or destroyed. On the other hand, God can be shown contempt when his own creature acts in a way that reflects badly on the Creator, as artists are disgraced by a poor, shoddy or defective piece of work they have done. Conversely, when people show kindness to the needy God is honored in two ways: first, because God's creation (the needy) is esteemed and cared for; second, because his creation (the kind persons) reflects in their behavior the kindness of the God who created them. In either event God's image in us gives us a capacity to honor or defame God by our own actions toward others.

Question 5. Fair-weather friends flock to the one who has a reputation for generosity. Naturally this complicates the giver's capacity to use discernment in his or her giving, as those who come around will, no doubt, have many compelling things to advise. Another problem arises if your reputation goes to your head because of the adulation you receive for your generosity. Jesus' advice is best here: "But when you give to the needy, do not let your left hand know what your right hand is doing, so that your giving may be in secret. Then your Father, who sees what is done in secret, will reward you" (Mt 6:3-4).

Question 7. It's startling enough to think that God would accept a loan in the first place. On this view God intends to meet the poor person's need, but this happens as we meet that need in his place, thereby "lending" to God—deploying our resources for his purposes. If you want to "loan" God something, then give to those to whom God would give. How we give to the needy is affected by this—we give with no strings attached; we are not to look to the needy person for recompense or even gratitude.

Question 8. Some people seem to think it is sub-Christian to give with the expectation of reward. But the Bible makes clear that generous saints are God's stewards, doing his will and fulfilling his purposes. It would be unjust if God were not to reward his faithful stewards!

Question 9. The answer is maybe yes and maybe no. Use this question to resurface, to clarify and to explore the applications of the proverbs in this study, along with any other giving principles that surfaced during the discussion. Two boundaries need to be maintained. First of all, legitimate needs exist that far exceed any individual's ability to meet them. Accordingly, we shouldn't feel guilty for not meeting all the needs that exist (a guilt which some solicitations seek to inflame). We must also avoid dereliction of already existing duties toward our family, parents, children or whatever. On the other hand, we shouldn't point to our inability to meet all needs as an excuse for failing to meet some. Proverbs 21:13 clearly warns us against deliberately turning away from the needy. The wisest course is to cultivate a habit of giving. A project involving those in the discussion group is a useful way to end this study.

Question 10. Look for two things as a minimal deployment of the wisdom of these proverbs. First, committing a discrete amount of our resources to assisting the poor will ensure that we are doing something with consistency. If the widow can give her two mites, none of us can protest that we have nothing to give. Second, we should look for someone in our vicinity to assist—someone we can see, touch and talk to. This will allow us to see firsthand the results of our giving. This "feedback" will foster a shrewdness in evaluating the opportunities for "giving 'at a distance" through charitable agencies.

Study 10. Proverbs 11:3; 14:12; 15:22; 16:9; 21:5, 31; 27:1. Planning the Future.

Purpose: To learn effective planning techniques so that our lives can be more fruitful and trouble free.

Questions 1-2. Proverbs 14:12 affirms our inadequacy to make infallible judgments, and Proverbs 27:1 reminds us of our inadequate knowledge. Even a course of action that appears sound and safe may be deadly, and even our good plans may be overturned.

These questions serve primarily to free up the thinking of the group, using the proverbs themselves as a launching point. Be alert for specific situations mentioned which might be reexamined later in the discussion in light of specific proverbs.

Question 3. Characteristics which enhance planning: integrity (11:13), personal responsibility (16:9; 21:31), diligence (21:5). Characteristics which hinder planning: duplicity (11:3), hastiness (21:5), arrogance (27:1).

Question 4. If planning were merely a matter of gathering information and making projections, then machines might do the job adequately. (Indeed for planning where information alone is significant, computers are rapidly taking the place of human planners.) But planning also involves factors such as goals, means and interests which compete with the plans we make. So moral standards and choices rise quickly to the surface, and a planner's character becomes a chief factor in the plans that are made.

Question 5. A counselor in Proverbs is anyone who is competent to offer advice in the area where advice is needed. A car mechanic, for example, might counsel you concerning odd noises in your car but not about odd noises in your stomach.

One consults a counselor for two things: knowledge of a subject area and experience with planning or problem solving in that area. It is extremely unlikely that one person will have all knowledge and wisdom. Consequently, to multiply counselors is to multiply the reservoir of knowledge and experience on which we may draw to make our plans.

Question 6. As a diligent planner you are not hasty. In planning the picnic you'll take as much time as necessary to explore all the details, to anticipate problems before they arise, and to make contingency plans. Because the project is complex, you must insure that location, food, drinks, games and game equipment, and transportation are all thought through. Diligence makes you plan for bad weather and first aid supplies. Diligence causes you to recruit helpers, to instruct them carefully in their responsibilities and then to monitor their work so it's done on time. Diligence, then, is thoroughness in attention to detail and in executing the plans that are made.

Questions 7-8. First, a theist will consult God's declared purposes wherever possible, especially as they are available in the Bible. If our plans oppose God's plans, God's wishes or God's character, we will abandon them (if we are wise). On the other hand, where we can plan in such a way as to align our purposes with God's, the likelihood of success is enhanced. Second, the wise person will pray. Beyond making plans, we should petition the One who can make any plan succeed or fail. Third, our personal integrity is always a guide in a universe that God has made and over which he rules (see Joseph's career as an example).

Question 9. Proverbs such as 16:9 and 21:31 juxtapose God's sovereignty and human responsibility. The proverbs do not attempt to reconcile their supposed inconsistencies. Rather, they simply affirm them side by side (as does the New Testament in several places; see especially Jn 1:12-13; Phil 2:12-13), thereby insisting that neither negates the other.

Proverbs 16:9 affirms that even the steps of a person's course are determined by God. But this in no way reduces one's need or responsibility to make plans. Proverbs 21:31 credits God for a victory in battle, but this does not mean the horse does not need to be prepared. God's sovereignty cannot discourage planning. For those who know God and trust him, his sovereignty can only enhance their planning for the future.

William Mouser has a Th.M. from Dallas Seminary with a specialization in Old Testament and Semitic languages. He is currently the director of the International Council for Gender Studies and lives near Dallas, Texas, with his wife and three daughters.